LEE CANTER'S

**HOMEWORK WITHOUT TEARS
FOR TEACHERS®**

PRACTICE HOMEWORK

Grades 1-3

A Publication of Lee Canter & Associates Inc.

Staff Writers

Patricia Ryan Sarka
Marcia Shank

Illustrator

Patty Briles

Editorial Staff

Marlene Canter
Carol Provisor
Kathy Winberry

Design

Pam Thomson

© 1989 Lee Canter & Associates Inc.
P. O. Box 2113, Santa Monica, CA 90406
(213) 395-3221 (800) 262-4347

ISBN 0-939007-26-6

Printed in the United States of America
First printing May 1989

Contents

About Homework Without Tears®

Lee Canter's Homework Without Tears is a comprehensive program that helps everyone—**teacher, students** and **parents**—learn to deal successfully with homework. The goal of the Homework Without Tears program is to give each of the three parties involved the tools they need to make homework an arena for success instead of a source of problems.

Teachers learn how to:

Communicate the importance of homework to students.
Assign more meaningful homework.
Show students how to do the homework.
Make homework creative and exciting.
Motivate students to do their best work.
Involve parents in the homework process.
Solve the most difficult homework problems.

Parents learn how to:

Emphasize the importance of homework to their children.
Give their children appropriate help.
Motivate children to do homework to the best of their ability.
Work with the teacher to solve homework problems.

Students learn how to:

Choose a time and a place to do homework.
Do homework on their own.
Motivate themselves to do their best work.
Utilize study skills to work more effectively.

When teachers, parents and students work together, homework can be a positive experience. The materials in the Homework Without Tears program have been designed to enhance and maximize everyone's efforts in the homework process.

This book, *Practice Homework*, reflects and expands upon a vital aspect of the Homework Without Tears program—the importance of giving appropriate homework assignments. Keep in mind that the ultimate quality of your homework program—and its benefit to your students—depends upon the effectiveness of the homework assignments you give.

Using Practice Homework Reproducibles

Practice homework is assigned so that students can review and practice specific skills or materials learned in class. The open-ended worksheets in this book have been created to provide you with varied, appropriate practice homework formats that are applicable for many skill areas. These formats include cut and paste, fill-in, completion, color-coding and more. Use these worksheets for everything from alphabet matching to simple multiplication facts practice. Examples and suggestions for each format are given at the beginning of each new section.

Read through the entire book to familiarize yourself with the variety of homework formats available to you. Choose a worksheet that fits your homework needs. Carefully remove it from the book and make a photocopy of the page. Return the original to the book. Using a fineline felt-tipped pen (preferably black), write in the specific direction you want your students to follow. Then use this page to make copies of the homework assignment for each student in your class. File this page for future use.

Once you have given complete and concise instructions to your students, hand out the assignment sheets. Give students ample time to ask questions concerning the assignment. When the homework assignments are turned in, make sure to grade or comment on each assignment.

Guidelines for Assigning More Effective Homework Practice

Keep the following points in mind when assigning practice homework:

- Don't give practice assignments if students do not need to practice that skill.

- Make sure that the practice assignment covers material learned in class.

- Assign practice homework only after you have determined that the student can do the work with reasonable success. Don't expect parents to "teach" skills to their children.

- Make sure a practice assignment focuses on a particular skill.

- Don't overdo drill assignments. Keep in mind that students who already grasp a concept don't need to practice, and would be better served and challenged by other types of homework. (Example: Why ask a student who already knows how to spell a word to write it ten times?) Likewise, students who don't understand a concept will just be reinforcing errors.

Tips for Improving the Effectiveness of Practice Homework*

Assigning practice homework that matches your students' varied abilities and also raises their level of thinking need not require greater amounts of teacher preparation time. You can still give textbook assignments and utilize supplemental and workbook worksheets. However, *how* you use these materials is one of the keys to assigning more effective homework.

The suggestions listed below will give you ideas for using textbooks and workbooks creatively and at the appropriate level. You will notice that all of these suggestions have been incorporated into specific *Practice Homework* worksheets. Examples appear on the introductory pages of each section.

- Instead of assigning all students the same 20-problem math page, have each student select 3 to 5 problems on the page that show what they are able to do. (See page 9, or use any of the formats in the Fill-Ins section.)

- Set a time limit that each student is expected to spend on a homework assignment and accept the number of problems the student does in that time. Have a parent signature verify the time. (See page 12.)

- Instead of assigning 20 math problems on a page, have students do the top 3, middle 3, and bottom 3. (See page 10.)

- Instead of defining spelling words, have students use the words in sentences, a poem or a creative story. (See pages 16 and 19.)

- Have students select 5 words (for example) from a story they have read in their reading book. Give them specifics for choosing these words: words that describe how people feel; words that describe how things look; words that describe how things move, etc. If appropriate, have students write the words in alphabetical order. (See pages 17 and 18.)

- After reading a story in the reader, ask students to draw a picture of a different ending to the story. (See page 20.)

These tips have been taken from Lee Canter's Homework Without Tears for Teachers, *Grades 1-3.*

Name _____ Date _____

Math Whiz

Select __10__ problems from page __126__ in your math book that show what you are able to do. Write and solve the problems in the space below.

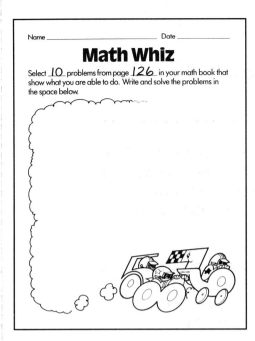

Name _____ Date _____

Hamburger Math

Do any __2__ problems from the top, middle, and bottom of page __15__ of your math book.

Name _____ Date _____

Half-and-Half Math

Do problems __9–15__ on page __81__ in your math book.

On the back of this page, write down __5__ more problems of your own. Make sure that the problems are the same kind that you did on the front of the worksheet. Solve the problems.

Math Masters

In a first-, second-, or third-grade classroom you may have many students with a wide span of math skills that require practicing. The worksheets in this section will allow you to individualize these practice skills, and thus improve the effectiveness of your homework assignments. The Practice Homework math formats make it easy! On most worksheets, you just fill in the number of problems to be completed and the page number. Your students do the rest! Here are a few of the wide range of math skills requiring practice in the primary grades:

- reads and writes numbers from 1 to 99 (depending on grade)
- identifies even and odd numbers
- counts by twos to 20 and fives and tens to 100
- counts backward from 10
- finds sums through 20
- knows addition facts through 18
- performs column addition (three 1-digit addends, sums through 18)
- adds 2 numbers, up to 2 digits, with and without regrouping
- subtracts 1-digit numbers from minuends through 18
- subtracts 2-digit numbers with and without regrouping
- identifies a whole, a half, one-fourth and one-third of a whole
- writes a fraction for a part of a whole
- identifies basic geometric shapes
- reads clock to specify time on the hour, the 1/2 hour, and 1/4 hour
- Identifies and names penny, nickel, dime and quarter
- counts and states value of coins from 1 cent to $1.00
- writes a number sentence to describe a real-life situation
- makes up a real life problem from a number sentence
- adds and subtracts sums in money problems up to $9.99

A sample practice application is given for each worksheet. You will be able to think of many more ways to use each format that will fit your homework learning objectives.

Math Whiz

This worksheet allows the student to choose specific problems from a textbook that show what he or she is able to do. Just fill in the page number and number of problems you want the students to do. Students perform all work on the worksheet.

Hamburger Math

Once again students are allowed to choose the problems—but this time they must choose problems from the top, middle and bottom of the page.

Half-and-Half Math

This assignment requires the students to do some specific problems from the textbook. Then, on the reverse side of the worksheet, the student is to create several more problems of his or her own using the same concept.

(Continued on back)

Tick-Tock Math

Do as many problems as you can in 10 minutes from page 54 in your math book.
Show your work in the space below.

Start time: _____ Finish time: _____
Number completed: _____ Parent signature: _____

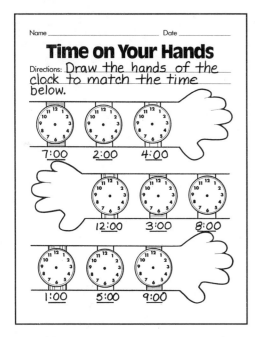

Time on Your Hands

Directions: Draw the hands of the clock to match the time below.

7:00   2:00   4:00

12:00   3:00   8:00

1:00   5:00   9:00

Tick-Tock Math

Students can race against the clock (with a parent as the timekeeper) on the Tick-Tock Math worksheet. Have the parent sign the completed paper.

Time on Your Hands

Is your class learning to tell time? Use the Time on Your Hands worksheet to practice reading and writing time on the hour, half and quarter hours.

Name _____ Date _____

Math Whiz

Select _____ problems from page _____ in your math book that show what you are able to do. Write and solve the problems in the space below.

Name _____ Date _____

Hamburger Math

Do any _____ problems from the top, middle, and bottom of page _____ of your math book. Show your work below.

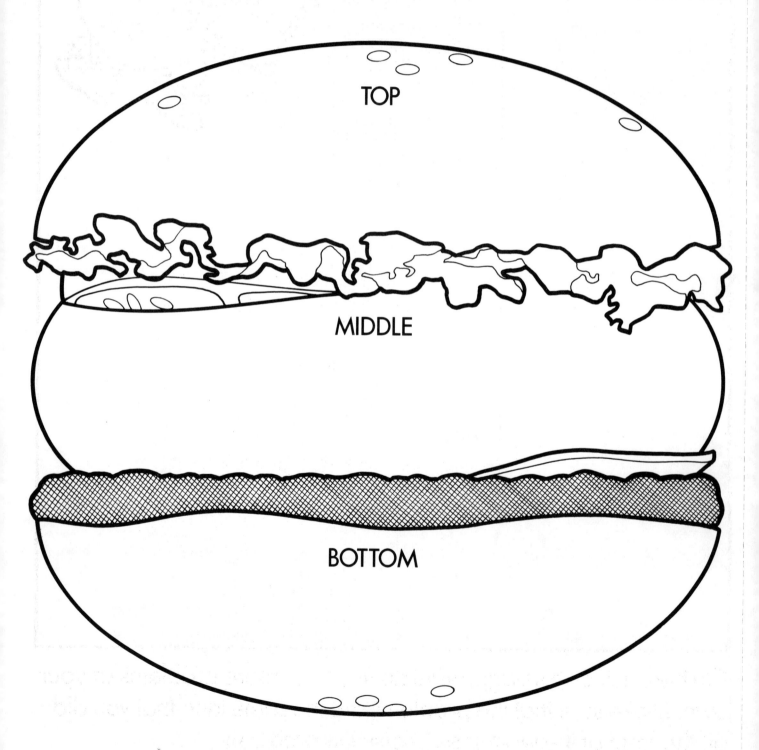

TOP

MIDDLE

BOTTOM

Name _____ Date _____

Half-and-Half Math

Do problems _____ on page _____
in your math book.

On the back of this page, write down _____ more problems of your
own. Make sure that the problems are the same kind that you did
on the front of the worksheet. Solve the problems.

Tick-Tock Math

Do as many problems as you can in _____

minutes from page _____ in your math book.

Show your work in the space below.

Start time: _____ Finish time: _____

Number completed: _____ Parent signature: _____

Name _____ Date _____

Time on Your Hands

Directions: _____

_____

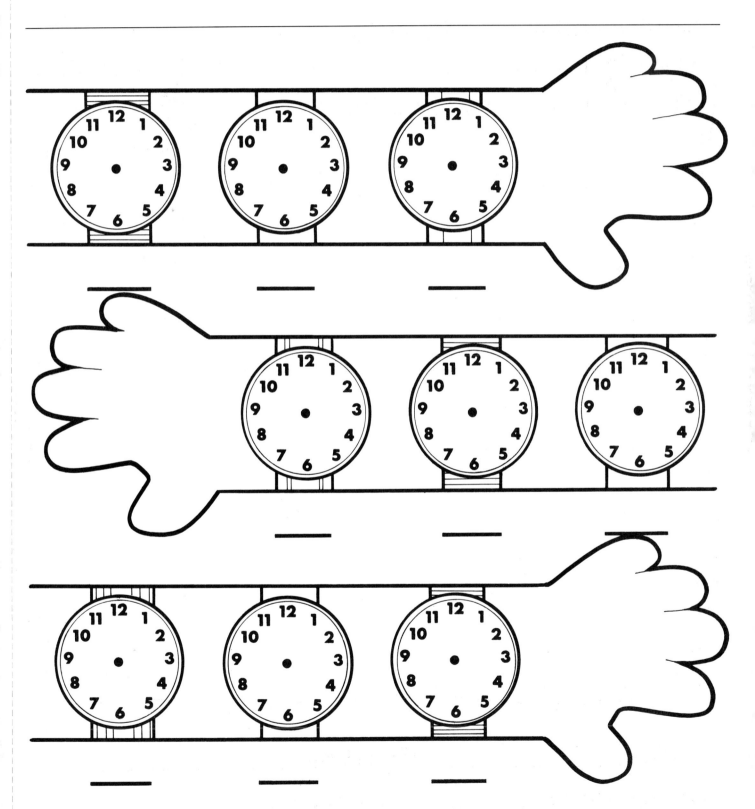

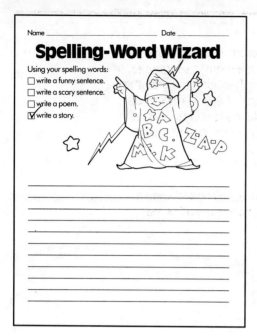

Working with Words

Spelling, vocabulary and handwriting homework make up a large portion of practice assignments given to younger students. Use the worksheets in this section as alternatives to workbook pages. You can use each format over and over again, changing the specific assignment to meet your homework goals.

A sample practice application is given for each worksheet. You will be able to think of many more ways to use each format that will fit your specific homework learning objectives.

Spelling-Word Wizard

Have students use their spelling words to write a funny or scary sentence, a poem, or a story. You choose the assignment or let the student select it.

Star Search

In conjunction with home or silent reading, have students find words from a story that: show action, describe feelings, contain silent letters, have the magic "e," etc.

Oink! Oink!

This 2-part worksheet is perfect for spelling and vocabulary word practice. Have students choose 8 words from a story and then write them in alphabetical order.

Other options:

Choose 8 words from a story that describe people.
Choose 8 words from a story that describe things.
Choose 8 words from a story that show action.

Name _____ Date _____

Dino-Mite!

Directions: Use a dictionary to define any 4 words in the dinosaur bone.

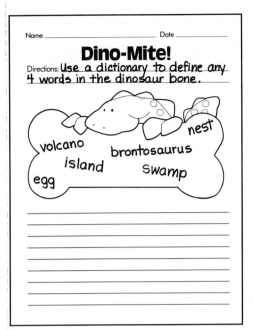

volcano
nest
brontosaurus
island
swamp
egg

_____
_____
_____
_____
_____
_____
_____
_____

Name _____ Date _____

Write and Draw

Directions: Write a story about your family. Draw a picture.

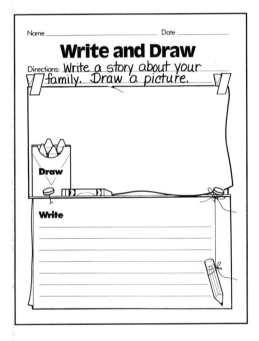

Draw

Write

Dino-Mite!

Write several spelling or vocabulary words in Dino's bone. Students can then define the words, use them in sentences, or create a prehistoric poem or story. Another option: Inside the bone have students write spelling words they misspelled on the trial test. The assignment is to write these words several times each, using the "write, close your eyes, spell it aloud, open your eyes, write it again" method.

Write and Draw

This worksheet is perfect for writing new endings to known stories or poems. Students illustrate on the top half of the worksheet and write on the bottom.

Name _____   Date _____

Spelling-Word Wizard

Using your spelling words:

☐ write a funny sentence.

☐ write a scary sentence.

☐ write a poem.

☐ write a story.

☐ _____ .

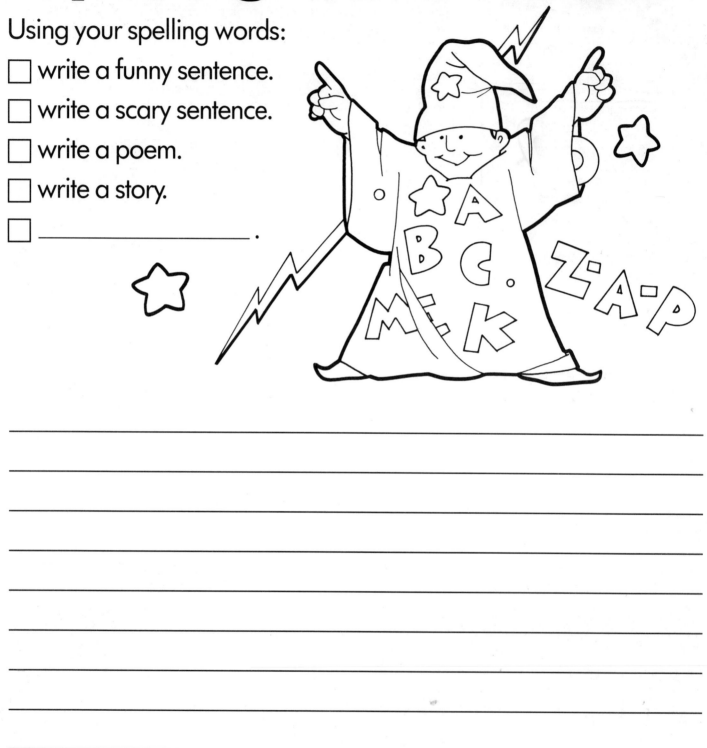

_____

_____

_____

_____

_____

_____

_____

_____

Name _____ Date _____

Star Search

Read pages _____ in your reader. Then, in each star,

write a word _____ .

Name _____ Date _____

Oink! Oink!

Directions: _____
_____ .

Name _____ Date _____

Dino-Mite!

Directions: _____

_____

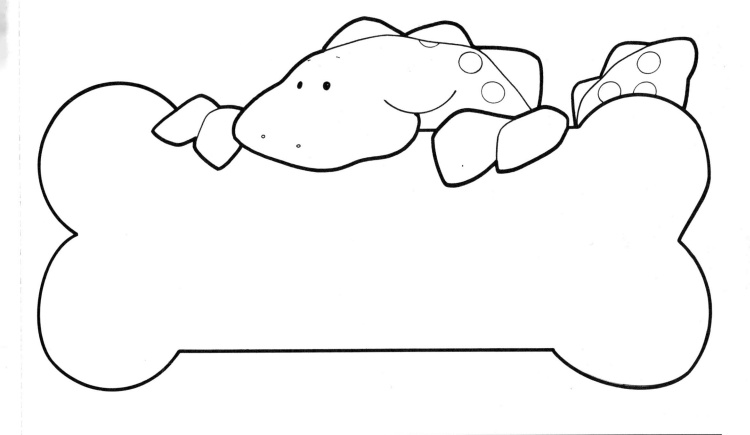

_____

_____

_____

_____

_____

_____

_____

Name _____ Date _____

Write and Draw

Directions: _____

Draw

Write

_____
_____
_____
_____
_____
_____
_____

Name _____ Date _____

Teddy Bear Time

Directions: *Write 8 words that describe your favorite stuffed animal.*

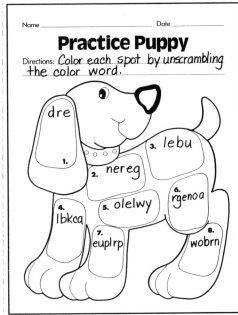

Name _____ Date _____

Practice Puppy

Directions: *Color each spot by unscrambling the color word.*

dre

3. lebu

1.

2. nereg

6. rgenoa

4. lbkca

5. olelwy

7. euplrp

8. wobrn

Name _____ Date _____

Mr. Turtle

Directions: *Number these words in ABC order.*

1. _ bat 2. _ cut 3. _ fish _ hat
   _ bus   _ can   _ feet   _ hen
   _ big   _ crab   _ flag   _ house

5. _ pill 6. _ sun 7. _ race 8. _ video
   _ pen   _ star   _ red   _ van
   _ pump   _ silk   _ ripe   _ vent

© 1989 Lee Canter & Associates Inc.

Teacher's Pets

These pets will make practice homework assignments a truly pleasant experience for your students. Parts of the pet bodies have been numbered. Students will write their practice answers inside the numbered areas. Spaces can also be used to color-code answers. These perky pets are especially suited for practicing these primary language arts and math skills:

Language Arts

* matches letters—uppercase to uppercase, lowercase to lowercase
* recognizes alphabet, uppercase and lowercase
* identifies initial consonant sounds
* identifies short vowel sounds
* identifies consonant digraphs: **sh   ch   th   wh   qu**
* counts syllables in 1- or 2-syllable words
* makes plurals: regular **s, es, ves**
* knows the contractions for **not, am, will**
* recognizes the basic sight words
* recognizes synonyms, antonyms
* classifies information
* arranges information in sequence
* alphabetizes to first and second letter
* follows simple written directions

Math

* finds sums through 20
* knows addition facts through 18
* subtracts 1-digit numbers from minuends through 18
* identifies basic geometric shapes
* reads clock to specify time on the hour, the 1/2 hour, and 1/4 hour

A sample practice application is given for each worksheet. You will be able to think of many more ways to use each format that will fit your specific homework learning objectives.

Teddy Bear Time

Directions: *If the two letters match, color the space blue. If the two letters do not match, color the space yellow.*

Practice Puppy

Directions: *Find the sum for each problem.*

Mr. Turtle

Directions: *Write a synonym for each word in the turtle's shell.*

Name _____ Date _____

Teddy Bear Time

Directions: _____

_____

Name _____ Date _____

Practice Puppy

Directions: _____
_____

Name _____ Date _____

Mr. Turtle

Directions: _____

_____

Spin a Web of Super Work!

Directions: *Write 2 words with the same final consonant as the first word.*

crop
bus
tail
bib
man
star
trap
bread

Here's the Scoop!

$$\begin{array}{r} 17 \\ 18 \\ +14 \end{array}$$

$$\begin{array}{r} 16 \\ 11 \\ +25 \end{array}$$

$$\begin{array}{r} 19 \\ 25 \\ +17 \end{array}$$

$$\begin{array}{r} 24 \\ 10 \\ +17 \end{array}$$

Directions: *Add the numbers in the scoops. Write the sum on the cone.*

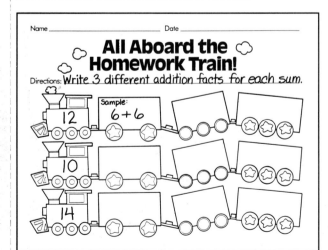

All Aboard the Homework Train!

Directions: *Write 3 different addition facts for each sum.*

12

Sample:
6 + 6

10

14

Add-Ons

These pages are very versatile. Use them in conjunction with book work or as self-contained worksheets. Students write their answers in the cars of the train, the scoops on the cones, or the lines on the spider's web. These worksheets are particularly applicable for practicing these math and language arts skills:

Language Arts
- supplies rhyming words
- supplies words with initial consonant sounds
- supplies words with same short vowel sounds
- supplies words with the same hard and soft sounds of **c** and **g**
- identifies and makes compound words
- matches words to given meanings
- writes synonyms, antonyms
- arranges information in sequence
- alphabetizes to first and second letter
- writes contractions from paired words and writes paired words from contractions
- selects correct prefixes: **un**, **pre**, **dis**
- selects appropriate suffixes: **s**, **es**, **ed**, **ing**, **er**, **est**

Math
- writes various addition and subtraction problems for a particular sum or difference
- performs columnar addition, with and without regrouping
- orders numbers from smallest to largest
- writes a fraction for a part of a whole
- identifies and makes basic geometric shapes
- counts and states value of coins from 1 cent to $1.00
- adds and subtracts sums in money problems up to $9.99
- writes single-digit subtraction problems with the same difference

A sample practice application is given for each worksheet. You will be able to think of many more ways to use each format that will fit your homework learning objectives.

Spin a Web of Super Work

Directions: *Write three words that rhyme with each word in the spider's web.*

Here's the Scoop!

Directions: *Write a subtraction problem in 2 scoops whose answer is the number in the cone.*

All Aboard the Homework Train!

Directions: *Find three words from each page of your story that describe how things look. Write them in the train's cars.*

Name _____ Date _____

Spin a Web
of Super Work!

Directions: _____

_____

Name _____ Date _____

Here's the Scoop!

Directions: _____

_____

_____

_____

Name _____

Date _____

All Aboard the Homework Train!

Directions:

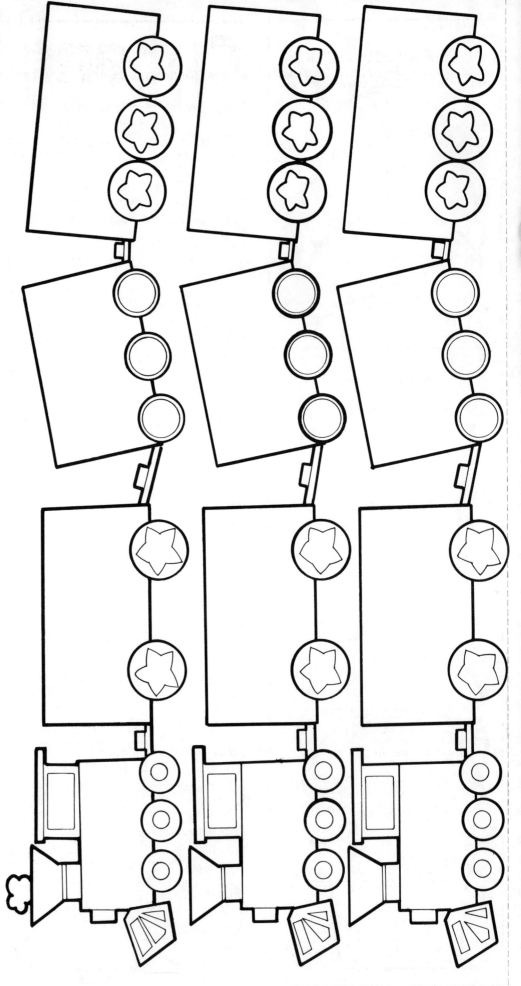

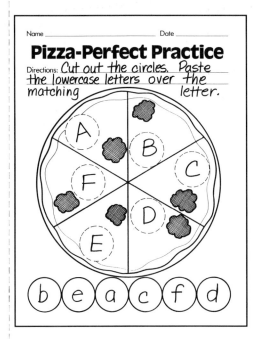

Pizza-Perfect Practice

Directions: Cut out the circles. Paste the lowercase letters over the matching letter.

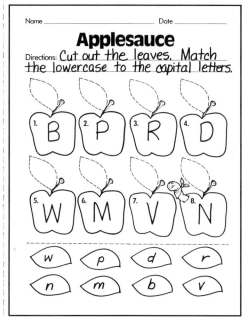

Applesauce

Directions: Cut out the leaves. Match the lowercase to the capital letters.

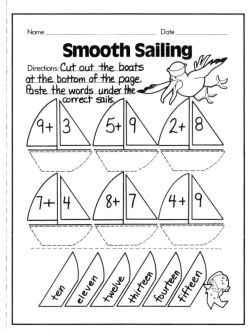

Smooth Sailing

Directions: Cut out the boats at the bottom of the page. Paste the words under the correct sails.

Cut and Paste

These cut-and-paste activities are perfect for all students in primary grades. Not only do they practice the fine motor skill of cutting, they also provide practice in basic skills. Those students who are not yet writing can use these pages for matching activities. For those students who can write, these worksheets provide a fun alternative for paper and pencil work. These are just a few language arts and math skills that can be used in conjunction with these worksheets:

Language Arts

- matches letters—uppercase to uppercase, lowercase to lowercase
- identifies initial consonant sounds
- identifies short vowel sounds
- identifies short and long vowel sounds
- identifies correct plural ending **-s** and **-es**
- supplies rhyming words
- identifies regular vowel digraphs: **ai ea ee ie oa ay oo**
- identifies consonant digraphs: **sh ch th wh qu**
- identifies the dipthongs: **aw au oi oy ou ow**
- counts syllables in 1-, 2-, and 3-syllable words
- knows the abbreviations: Mr., Ms., Ave., Blvd., Mrs., St., Dr.
- matches words to given meanings
- recognizes synonyms, antonyms

Math

- identifies products for basic multiplication facts
- finds sums through 20
- finds differences through 20
- knows addition facts through 18
- computes sums and differences from simple word problems
- reads clock to specify time on the hour, the 1/2 hour, and 1/4 hour
- adds and subtracts sums in money problems up to $9.99

A sample practice application is given for each worksheet. You will be able to think of many more ways to use each format that will fit your homework learning objectives.

Pizza-Perfect Practice

Directions: *Read the word in each pizza slice. Decide if the word has a long or short vowel sound. Cut and paste the correct pepperoni on each slice.*

Applesauce

Directions: *Read the word in each apple. Say the plural form of the word. Cut and paste the leaf with the correct plural ending.*

Smooth Sailing

Directions: *Multiply the numbers in each sail. Cut and paste the correct product onto the boat.*

Name _____   Date _____

Pizza-Perfect Practice

Directions: _____

_____

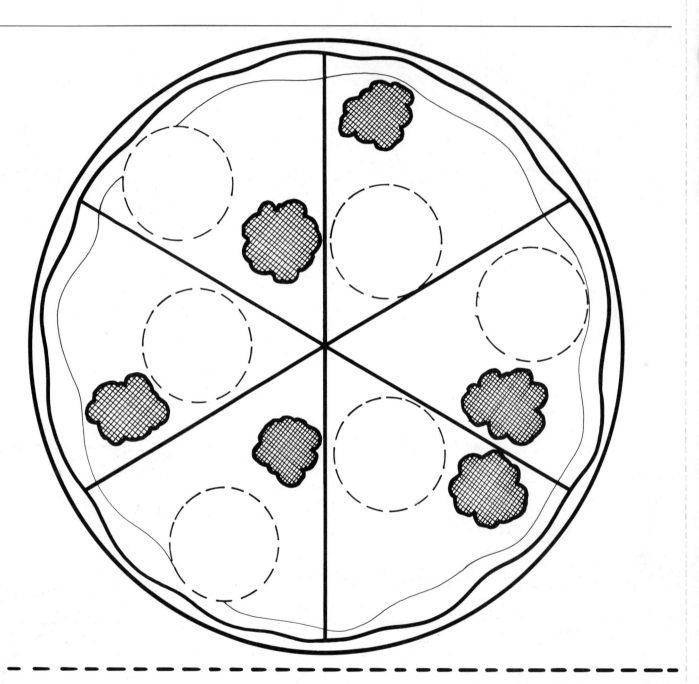

Name _____ Date _____

Applesauce

Directions: _____

_____

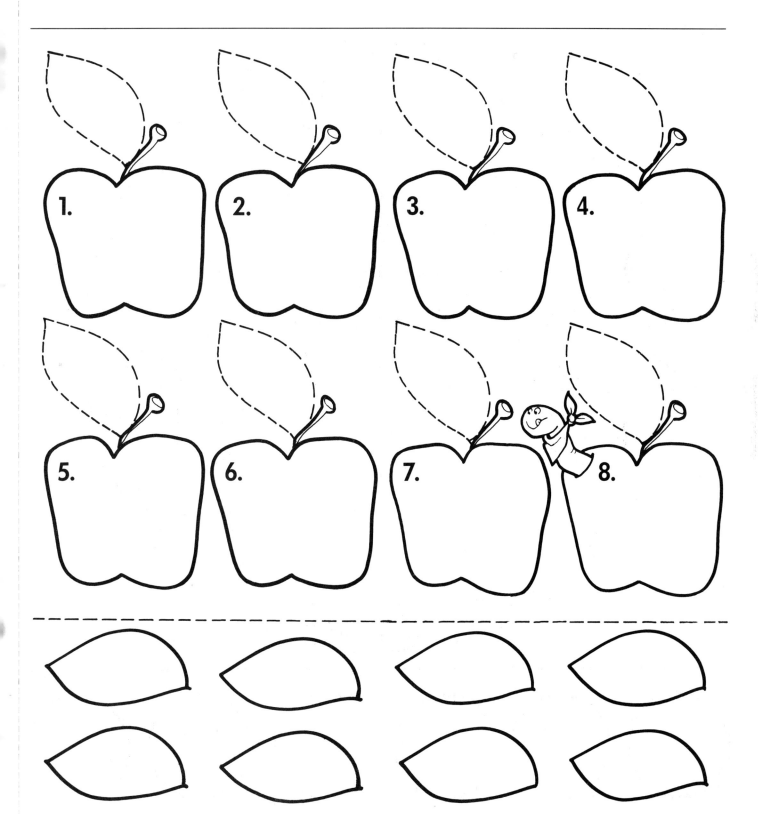

Name _____ Date _____

Smooth Sailing

Directions: _____

_____

_____

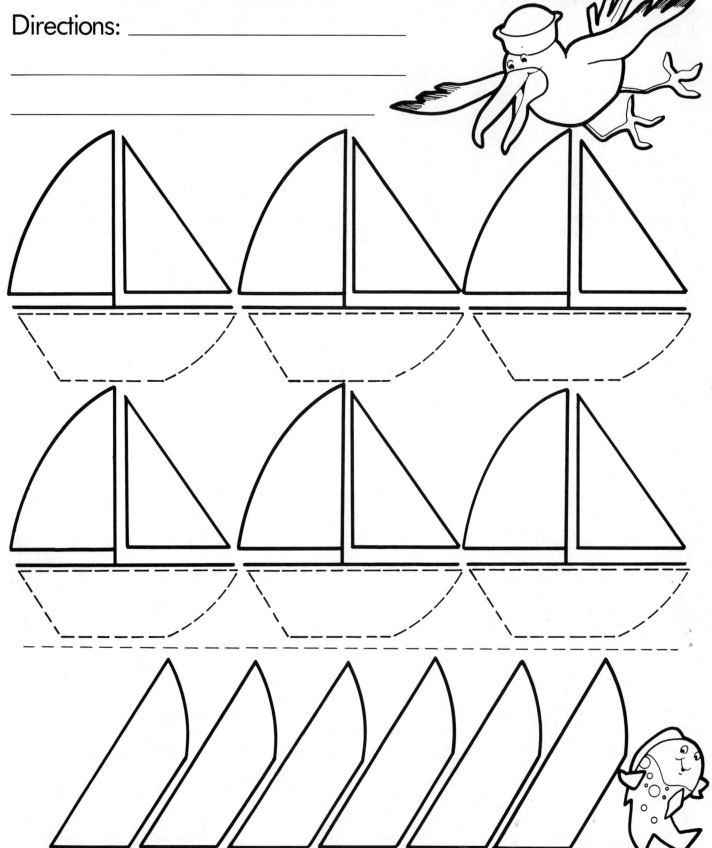

Drop in the Bucket

Directions: Write 4 words in each bucket that belong to the category on the paint.

vehicles | clothes | Colors
1. | 2. | 3.

games | relatives | pets
4. | 5. | 6.

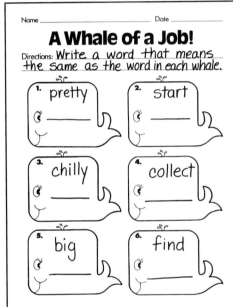

A Whale of a Job!

Directions: Write a word that means the same as the word in each whale.

1. pretty
2. start
3. chilly
4. collect
5. big
6. find

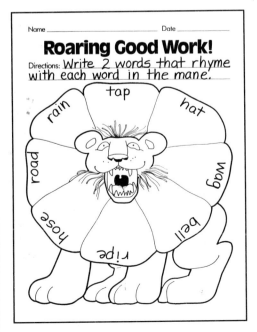

Roaring Good Work!

Directions: Write 2 words that rhyme with each word in the mane.

tap
rain
hat
road
wag
nose
bell
ripe

Fill-Ins

More is not always better when it comes to homework practice. To determine, for example, if students know how to perform addition problems with 2-digit regrouping, you do not need to overwhelm them with 30 or more homework problems. Ten well-chosen problems will give students enough practice for one night. Notice that several of the fill-in pages have spaces that are not numbered. Allow students to choose any 6 or 10 problems that show what they can do on a particular page of a book. Students fill in the problem or question numbers and show their work and answers in the spaces.

Here are several suggested skills for which these worksheets can be adapted for practice homework:

Language Arts

- supplies rhyming words
- identifies initial consonant sounds
- identifies short vowel sounds
- recognizes and reads words containing long vowel/final **e**
- identifies the hard and soft sounds of **c** and **g**
- identifies and makes compound words
- counts syllables in 1-, 2-, and 3-syllable words
- makes plurals: regular **s, es, ves**
- recognizes the basic sight words
- matches words to given meanings
- identifies main ideas
- classifies information
- alphabetizes to first and second letter
- writes a description using language related to size, shape, color, 5 senses
- writes a description of a person, place, thing or action
- locates words in a dictionary
- capitalizes the first letters in the name of days of week, special days, months, streets and cities
- selects or writes irregular noun plurals: children, mice, knives

Math

- counts by twos to 20 and fives and tens to 100
- finds sums through 20
- knows addition facts through 18
- identifies missing numbers in a sequence or pattern
- subtracts 1-digit numbers from minuends through 18
- writes a fraction for a part of a whole
- identifies and/or draws basic geometric shapes
- writes a number sentence to describe a real-life situation
- adds and subtracts sums in money problems up to $9.99

A sample application is given for each worksheet. These samples will give you an idea of the wide range of activities that can be created using the Fill-Ins worksheets. You will be able to think of many more ways to use each format that will fit your homework learning objectives.

(Continued on back)

Name _____ Date _____

Homonym **Hotel**

Directions: Write a homonym pair in each hotel window.

1. (Sample) there their	2.	3.
4.	5.	6.
7.	8.	

Drop in the Bucket

Directions: *Choose any 6 problems from page 38 in your math book. Write the answers on the paint buckets. Color the odd answers green. Color the even answers orange.*

A Whale of a Job!

Directions: *Fill in the missing numbers.*

Roaring Good Work!

Directions: *Read the story on pages 23 to 30 in your reading book. For each page, write the 2-syllable word that you find most difficult. Write the page number and the word on the lion's mane.*

_____ Hotel

This "hotel" worksheet can be named according to the skill to be practiced (for example: Homonym Hotel, Vocabulary Hotel or Handwriting Hotel). Fill in the rooms with the appropriate answers.

Directions: *Draw and color the shapes listed in each window.*

Name _____   Date _____

Drop in the Bucket

Directions: _____
_____

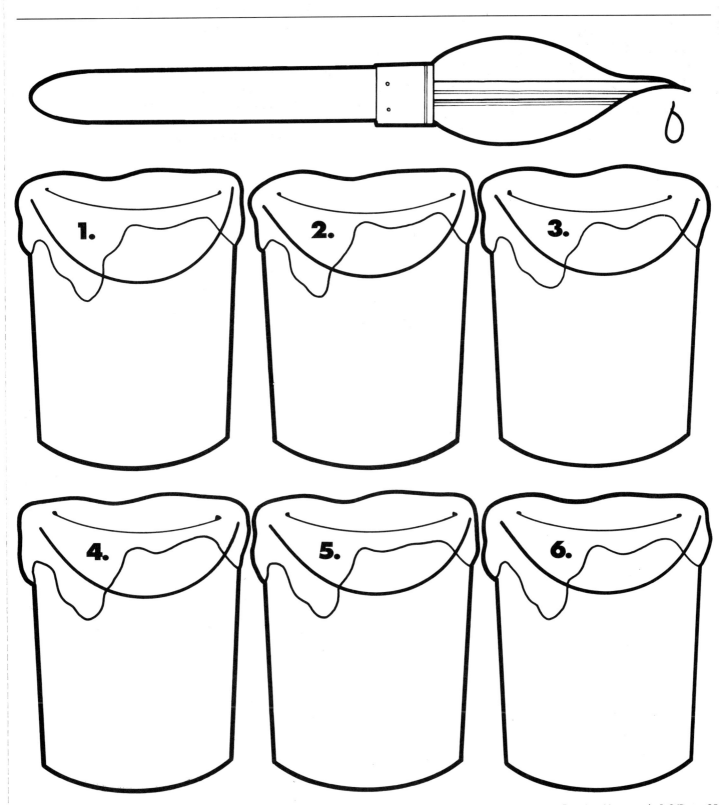

Name _____ Date _____

A Whale of a Job!

Directions: _____
_____

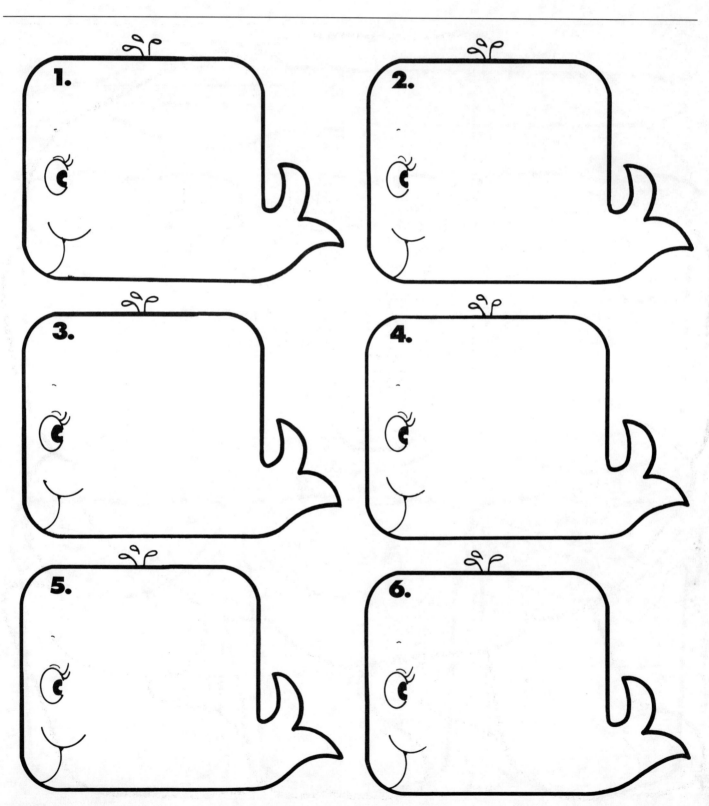

1.

2.

3.

4.

5.

6.

Name _____ Date _____

Roaring Good Work!

Directions: _____

_____

Name _____ Date _____

_____ **Hotel**

Directions: _____

_____

1.

2.

3.

4.

5.

6.

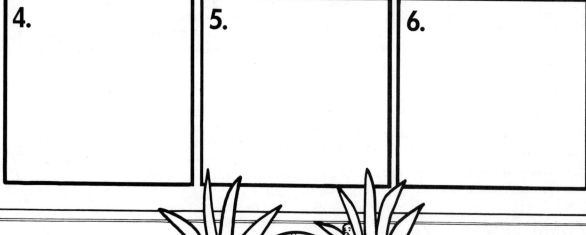

7.

8.

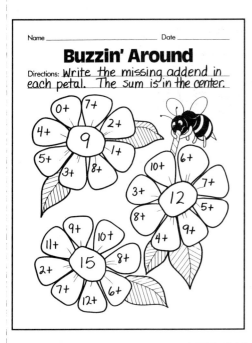

Buzzin' Around

Directions: Write the missing addend in each petal. The sum is in the center.

Gumball Machine

Directions: Write a vowel in each gumball. Color all the words you can read.

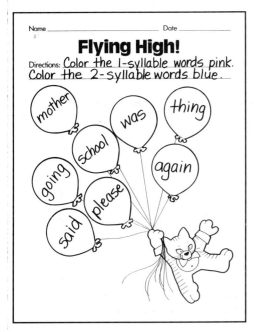

Flying High!

Directions: Color the 1-syllable words pink. Color the 2-syllable words blue.

Color Codes

Your students will need their crayons to complete these color-code practice sheets. You write in the words, math problems, or questions and answers. Students respond by coloring the petals, gumballs, or space ships in the appropriate colors.

Here is a list of skills that can be practiced using these worksheets:

Language Arts

- identifies non-rhyming from rhyming words
- chooses correct initial consonant sounds
- identifies matching letters—uppercase to uppercase, lowercase to lowercase
- identifies initial consonant sounds
- identifies short vowel sounds
- recognizes **cvc** words
- recognizes words containing long vowel/final **e**
- chooses correct initial consonant clusters
- chooses correct consonant digraphs:
  sh   ch   th   wh   qu
- identifies the hard and soft sounds of **c** and **g**
- chooses correct dipthongs to form new words:
  aw   au   oi   oy   ou   ow
- chooses correct 3-letter clusters to form new words:
  scr   spl   spr   str   thr   nch
- identifies compound words
- counts syllables in 1-, 2-, and 3-syllable words
- chooses correct regular plurals: **s, es, ves**
- chooses correct singular possessives
- identifies words that require capitalization
- recognizes correct contractions using **not, am, will**

Math

- identifies even and odd numbers
- identifies correct sums through 20
- adds 2 numbers, up to 2-digits, with and without regrouping
- identifies a whole, 1/2, 1/4 and 1/3 of a whole
- identifies basic geometric shapes
- identifies correct number sentences
- supplies correct sign: $<$, $>$, and $=$
- adds money with and without regrouping

A sample practice application is given for each worksheet. You will be able to think of many more ways to use each format that will fit your homework learning objectives.

Buzzin' Around

Directions: *Read the word in each petal. If the word always needs to be capitalized, color the petal orange. If the word only needs to be capitalized at the beginning of a sentence, color the petal yellow.*

(Continued on back)

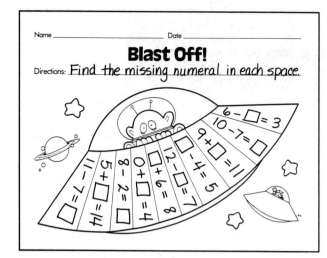

Name _____ Date _____

Blast Off!

Directions: Find the missing numeral in each space.

(equations on spaceship rays:)
$6 - \square = 3$
$10 - 7 = \square$
$9 + \square = 11$
$12 - \square = 8$
$\square - 4 = 5$
$0 + \square = 4$
$8 - 2 = \square$
$5 + \square = 7$
$11 - 7 = \square$
$\square = 14$

Gumball Machine

Directions: *Read the word in each gumball. If the word is a noun, color it blue. If the word is a pronoun, color it yellow. If the word is a verb, color it green.*

Flying High

Directions: *Look at the number in each balloon. If the number is even, color the balloon blue. If the number is odd, color the balloon yellow.*

Blast Off!

Directions: *Add the numbers. If the sum is less than $1.05, color the space yellow. If the sum is more than $1.05, color the space purple.*

Name _____ Date _____

Buzzin' Around

Directions: _____
_____

Name _____ Date _____

Gumball Machine

Directions: _____
_____

Name _____

Date _____

Blast Off!

Directions: _____

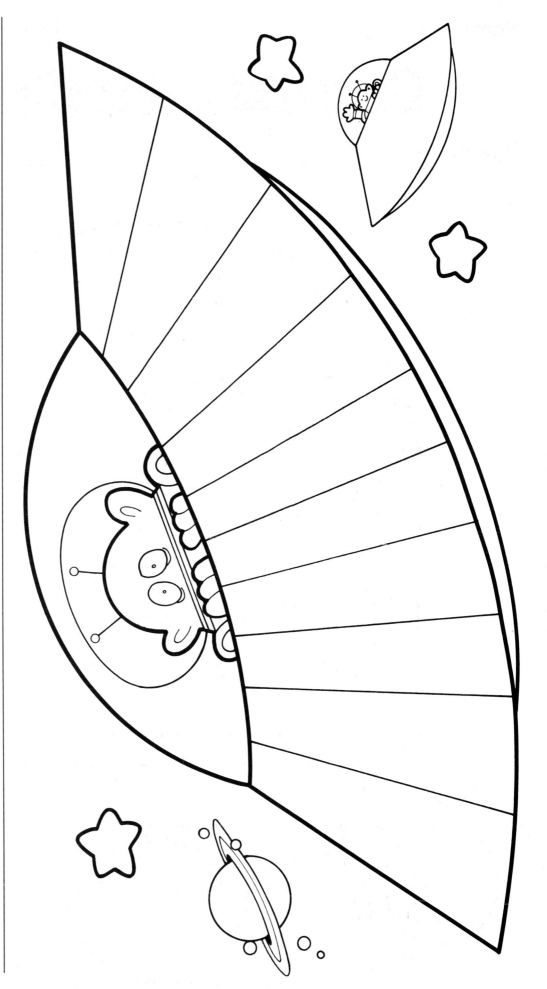

Name _____ Date _____

Flying High!

Directions: _____
_____

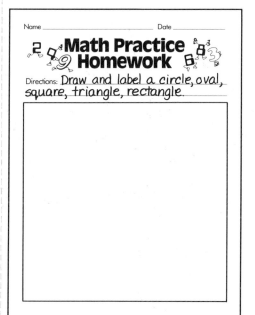

My Practice Homework

Name _____ Date _____

Directions: Write your name, address and telephone number.

Practice Homework

Name _____ Date _____

Directions: Write a friendly letter to your favorite character in your book.

practice makes perfect... practice makes perfect...
practice makes perfect... practice makes perfect...

Math Practice Homework

Name _____ Date _____

Directions: Draw and label a circle, oval, square, triangle, rectangle.

Practice Homework
for Writing and Computation

These open-ended practice worksheets are perfect for handwriting practice, math drill, and a variety of language arts activities. Here are just a few primary language arts and math skills that could be used in conjunction with these worksheets:

Language Arts

- writes uppercase and lowercase manuscript letters and numerals from a model
- writes first name and last name
- writes address and telephone number
- writes sentences using correct ending punctuation
- writes and recites jingles, poems, and rhymes
- hears and writes selected initial consonant and vowel sounds
- arranges information in sequence
- follows simple written directions
- writes stories of two or more sentences with a title

Math

- reads and writes numbers from 1 to 99 (depending on grade)
- identifies even and odd numbers
- counts backward from 10
- finds sums through 20
- knows addition facts through 18
- adds 2 numbers, up to 2 digits, with and without regrouping
- subtracts 2-digit numbers with and without regrouping
- identifies a whole, 1/2, 1/4 and 1/3

A sample practice application is given for each worksheet. You will be able to think of many more ways to use each format that will fit your homework learning objectives.

My Practice Homework

Sample Directions:

- *Write the lowercase letters of the alphabet in order.*
- *Write the numerals from 1 to 20 (by 2s).*

Practice Homework

Sample Directions:

- *Choose any 10 spelling words (vocabulary words). Look up each word in the dictionary. Write the guide words found on the dictionary page for each word.*
- *Copy any paragraph from the story in your reading book. Then circle the nouns, underline the verbs, and box the adjectives.*

Math Practice Homework

Sample Directions:

- *Draw 3 squares and 3 circles on the paper. Divide them into fractions and color as follows: 1/2, 1/4, 1/3, 1/1, 3/4, and 2/3.*
- *Write 2 story problems about animals. Illustrate each problem.*

Name _____ Date _____

My Practice Homework

Directions: _____

_____

- -
_____

- -
_____

- -
_____

- -
_____

- -
_____

- -
_____

- -
_____

Name _____ Date _____

Practice Homework

Directions: _____

_____

<table>
<tr><td rowspan="14" style="writing-mode: vertical-rl">practice makes perfect... practice makes perfect...</td><td></td><td rowspan="14" style="writing-mode: vertical-rl">practice makes perfect... practice makes perfect...</td></tr>
<tr><td>_____</td></tr>
<tr><td>_____</td></tr>
<tr><td>_____</td></tr>
<tr><td>_____</td></tr>
<tr><td>_____</td></tr>
<tr><td>_____</td></tr>
<tr><td>_____</td></tr>
<tr><td>_____</td></tr>
<tr><td>_____</td></tr>
<tr><td>_____</td></tr>
<tr><td>_____</td></tr>
<tr><td>_____</td></tr>
<tr><td>_____</td></tr>
</table>

practice makes perfect... practice makes perfect...

© 1989 Lee Canter & Associates Inc.

Name _____ Date _____

Math Practice Homework

Directions: _____

_____